The Mayflower Compact

E.J. CARTER

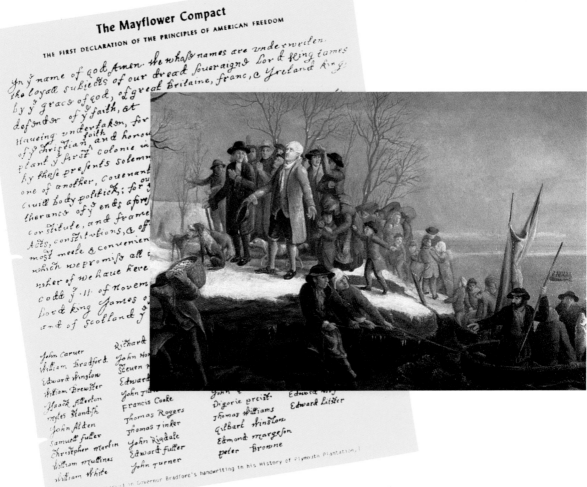

Heinemann Library
Chicago, Illinois

© 2004 Heinemann Library
an imprint of Capstone Global Library, LLC
Chicago, Illinois

Customer Service 888-454-2279

Visit our website at www.heinemannlibrary.com

Designed by Herman Adler Design
Photo research by Bill Broyles
Printed and bound in the United States of America,
Stevens Point, WI.

072012
006841CPS

Library of Congress Cataloging-in-Publication Data
Carter, E. J., 1971-
  The Mayflower Compact / E.J. Carter.
    p. cm. -- (Historical documents)
Summary: Discusses the history of the Pilgrims in
Massachusetts, the early government of the Plymouth
Colony, and the document known as the Mayflower
Compact.
Includes bibliographical references and index.
ISBN 1-4034-0803-3 (lib. bdg.) -- ISBN 1-978-4034-3432-6
(pbk.)
 1. Mayflower Compact (1620)--Juvenile literature. 2.
Pilgrims (New Plymouth Colony)--Juvenile literature. 3.
Mayflower (Ship)--Juvenile literature. 4. Massachusetts--
History--New Plymouth, 1620-1691--Juvenile literature. 5.
Massachusetts--Politics and
government--To 1775--Juvenile literature. [1. Mayflower
Compact (1620) 2. Pilgrims (New Plymouth Colony) 3.
Massachusetts--History--New Plymouth, 1620-1691.] I.
Title. II. Historical documents (Heinemann Library (Firm))
  F68.C33 2003
  974.4'02--dc21
                          2003008195

102011
006373RP

Acknowledgments
The author and publisher are grateful to the following for
permission to reproduce copyright material:

Cover photographs by (document) Massachusetts State
Library; (Mayflower) Burstein Collection/Corbis; (portraits,
T-B) North Wind Picture Archives, North Wind Picture
Archives, Kindra Clineff; (title bar) Corbis.

Title page (L-R) Massachusetts State Library, Pilgrim Hall
Museum; p. 4 Jason Hawkes/Corbis; p. 5 The Bridgeman
Art Library; pp. 6, 20, 25b, 43 Massachusetts State Library;
pp. 7, 8, 16, 17, 38 Burstein Collection/Corbis; pp. 9t, 13,
28t, 31, 33 Pilgrim Hall Museum; pp. 9b, 26, 32, 36, 37
Bettmann/Corbis; pp. 10, 15, 18b, 19, 21, 22, 23, 24, 25t,
30, 35t North Wind Picture Archives; p. 11 Gianni Dagli
Orti/Corbis; p. 18t Kindra Clineff; p. 28b Christie's Images/
Corbis; p. 29 British Library/The Art Archive; pp. 34, 39t
Corbis; p. 35b The Corcoran Gallery of Art/Corbis; p. 39b
Mark E. Gibson/Corbis; p. 40 National Archives and Records
Administration; p. 41 Angelo Hornak/Corbis; p. 42 Kevin
Fleming/Corbis; pp. 44, 45 Kevin Fleming/Corbis.

Special thanks to Derek Shouba for his help in the
preparation of this book.

Every effort has been made to contact copyright holders
of any material reproduced in this book. Any omissions
will be rectified in subsequent printings if notice is given
to the publisher.

Some words are shown in bold,
like this. You can find out what
they mean by looking in the glossary.

Contents

Recording Important Events

Throughout history, people have created documents so they will have a record of an important event. The documents may tell stories about how people lived, how significant discoveries were made, or what occurred during a war.

Documents that provide a historical record of something can be divided into two categories: **primary sources** and **secondary sources.**

Primary sources

When **historians** are studying what happened in the past, they prefer to use primary sources. This term refers to documents that provide a firsthand account of an event. Primary sources can include letters, diaries, newspaper articles, **pamphlets,** and other papers that were written by people who witnessed or were directly involved in an event.

Primary sources can also include official papers that were carefully planned, often with much discussion and argument. The people involved in the planning and writing of official papers were careful to make sure the words that went into the documents expressed exactly the thoughts and ideas they wanted them to. Official papers are a clear record of just what the authors intended to say.

This is a modern-day view of Plymouth Harbor in England. It is from this point that the **Pilgrims** sailed to the New World.

The Pilgrims landed in the New World at the start of winter—conditions were often cold and harsh. This print depicts what life may have been like at first for the Pilgrims.

Primary sources tell us, in the words of the people who lived during that time, what really happened. They are a kind of direct communication that has not been filtered through a lot of sources. Often, stories that are passed verbally from person to person change as they are told and retold. Facts become muddled and confused, and information is added or left out. Soon, the original story has completely changed.

This is why primary sources are important. Over time, facts can be changed or twisted, accidentally or on purpose, so unwritten accounts of what happened in the past can be incorrect. To find out what really happened and why, historians rely on printed or handwritten primary sources.

Secondary sources

Secondary sources are accounts of events written by people who have studied primary sources. They read letters, **journals,** and other firsthand accounts, then write their own version based on their research.

5

The Massachusetts State House

Because **primary sources** provide an important record of historical events, they are considered valuable. For that reason, the paper-and-ink documents are carefully handled and stored so that they will last a long time. Documents that are considered valuable records of United States history are kept in several different places.

Rediscovering the Mayflower Compact

A good example of a primary source is the Mayflower Compact. The Mayflower Compact was written in 1620, and for the next 150 years people mostly ignored it. It was not considered an especially important document and very few people had a chance to read it. Then in 1776, the United States declared its independence from Great Britain. After the **Revolutionary War,** the United States became a separate country with its own **constitution.**

This copy of the Mayflower Compact is from William Bradford's book, *Of Plymouth Plantation.* It is written in his own handwriting.

At that time, many people decided that the Mayflower Compact was an important part of U.S. history. It seemed to predict the **Declaration of Independence** and the U.S. Constitution. Suddenly, Americans became interested in reading, printing, and studying the Mayflower Compact to learn more about its role in U.S. history.

The first copy

The earliest known copy of the Mayflower Compact appears in William Bradford's book, *Of Plymouth Plantation*. This was a historical record of the **Pilgrims**' early years in Plymouth **Colony** between 1620 and 1646. Today this book is stored in the Massachusetts State House in Boston, Massachusetts. The State House is not just a museum—it is the place where the Massachusetts **legislature** meets and **debates** new laws. Most of the people who work at the State House are **senators** and representatives and their staffs. But the State House is also home to many important historical documents that concern Massachusetts history. The early colonial era and the Revolutionary War are especially important in Massachusetts. So the State House has many documents from those periods.

The old Massachusetts State House was the first to house the Mayflower Compact.

The Massachusetts State Library contains other important documents as well. These include the papers of important Massachusetts politicians, newspapers, photographs, city directories (before phone books came along), and maps. It also includes a large collection of **broadsides,** or printed announcements, from the eighteenth- and nineteenth-centuries. Broadsides could be anything from songs to advertisements to government announcements.

The Mayflower Compact

THE FIRST DECLARATION OF THE PRINCIPLES OF AMERICAN FREEDOM

Landing of the Pilgrims

In November 1620, after a four-month voyage across the Atlantic Ocean, the *Mayflower* sighted land. The **Pilgrims** had reached Cape Cod, Massachusetts, near what is now the city of Provincetown. Before actually going ashore, the men and women aboard the ship decided to take stock of their situation and prepare for the future. They planned out the kind of community they wanted to build. They knew that a dangerous environment awaited them on land.

Many Pilgrims were already weak from disease and from living packed together on the ship. Winter was approaching, and they knew winters in the New World were much colder than in Europe. Because it was already November, they would not be able to grow food to allow them to survive the winter. In a very short time they would have to build shelter to keep themselves warm, and find a supply of food to last through the winter. In fact, dozens of Pilgrims would die during that first winter.

The voyage

The *Mayflower* was a large cargo ship, 90 feet (27 meters) in length. Before its voyage to New England, it had been used for several years in the wine trade between England and France. During the 66-day voyage, the *Mayflower* frequently sailed in stormy weather. At one point, the ship's main beam cracked. It was repaired using a large iron screw.

After the initial shock of life in a new land, the Pilgrims that survived the first winter celebrated the first Thanksgiving.

The first form of government

The Pilgrims could not afford to argue amongst themselves. So before they came ashore, the men onboard the *Mayflower* wrote and signed a compact. They promised **loyalty** to the King of England and to their religion. They also vowed to work together to create a new society. This document later became known as the Mayflower Compact, and has sometimes been called the first form of government created in America.

The Mayflower Compact

DECLARATION OF THE PRINCIPLES OF AMERICAN FREED

9

The Protestant and the English Reformations

To understand what brought the **Pilgrims** to America, one must go back to the time of the **Protestant Reformation**. The Reformation began in Germany in 1519, when a **monk** named Martin Luther began criticizing the Catholic Church. Luther felt that the church had become too concerned with raising money and was not fulfilling its religious duties.

Martin Luther

Luther and Calvin

Luther quickly gathered many followers, and some of them urged him to break with the church and **found** a new religion or a new branch of Christianity. One of Luther's most important followers was John Calvin. He was born in France, but later moved to Geneva, Switzerland. Calvin used some of Luther's ideas to create a very strict, very **devout** religion that won many **converts** in France, Switzerland, Holland, Great Britain, and Scotland. The Calvinists tried to practice a very pure form of Christianity, avoiding anything they considered evil or **sinful.**

John Calvin

Although many Protestants—as the followers of Luther and Calvin came to be called—

Henry VIII

Henry VIII was born in Greenwich, England (near London), in 1491. He became king in 1509 when he was seventeen years old. He is known for his lavish lifestyle, cruelty, and six wives. However, his greatest influence on Great Britain was to separate the Church of England from the Roman Catholic Church. Henry VIII died in 1547.

lived in England and Scotland, they did not succeed in creating an official Protestant church at first. Eventually, Great Britain did become Protestant, but in an unusual way. Henry VIII was King of England and had been married to Catherine of Aragon for eighteen years. They did not have a male child to take over the throne after Henry died. Therefore, he wanted to divorce his wife and marry another woman.

A new church

The **pope,** however, refused to dissolve the marriage to Catherine. So Henry decided to create a new religious organization, the Anglican Church. In 1534, he claimed all church property for himself and forced the **clergy** to convert to his church. Now he could act as he wanted without first receiving the pope's blessing.

The Anglican Church, however, was only partially Protestant. The Calvinists were not entirely happy with Anglicanism. They began to call themselves **Puritans** because they wanted to practice a purer and simpler religion. Most of the men and women onboard the *Mayflower* shared the religious beliefs of the Puritans.

The Mayflower Compact
THE FIRST DECLARATION OF THE PRINCIPLES OF AMERICAN FREEDOM

The Separatists

Within the **Puritan** movement an even more **radical** group, known as the **Separatists,** began to appear in the late sixteenth century. Most Puritans were willing to live with the Anglican Church, hoping that it would slowly become more Calvinist. But the Separatists refused to have anything to do with it. They wanted to live entirely on their own, with their own church, their own schools, and their own government. British officials were willing to tolerate Puritans, but they banned Separatists and tried to put them in jail.

One of these Separatist groups was **founded** near the village of Scrooby, located in the north Midlands of Great Britain. The Scrooby **congregation** met on the **estate** of William Brewster until the year 1606, when the British government threatened to imprison its members. The Scrooby congregation decided to escape to the city of Leiden in Holland. Holland was a more Calvinist country and would allow the congregation to practice their religion.

For the next eleven years the Scrooby congregation lived in Holland peacefully, under the leadership of their pastor, John Robinson. But by 1620, they had decided to move on to the New World. There were three main reasons for the decision

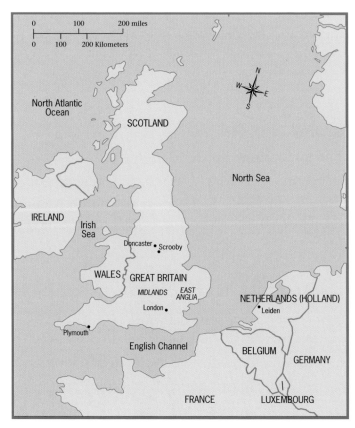

When pressure increased on the Separatist groups in Great Britain, the Scrooby congregation fled to Holland.

to move. First, they were afraid Holland was going to be invaded by Spain. Second, they thought that their children might eventually give up their strict Puritan religion, and start to mix

Isaac Allerton

Isaac Allerton was one of four people chosen to plan the trip to North America. He bought two ships, the *Speedwell* and the *Mayflower*. He supplied the ships with food, water, a crew of sailors, and everything else they needed for their voyage. Unfortunately, the *Speedwell* was leaky. At Plymouth, England, the group stopped and everyone piled onto the *Mayflower*. Once the Pilgrims arrived in North America, Allerton became a very important person. He often traveled back to England to get loans and **patents** to the land the Pilgrims had occupied.

with the rest of the people in Leiden. Finally, they were having trouble finding jobs.

John Robinson decided to send part of his congregation to the New World to spread the religion and make sure it survived. Isaac Allerton was put in charge of organizing the journey, and in the summer of 1620 the **Pilgrims** set off from Holland. They stopped at Plymouth, England, to get more supplies, and then left for the New World.

The *Speedwell* and the *Mayflower* were not at sea long before the *Speedwell* was forced back to Dartmouth Harbor in Plymouth for repairs.

The Mayflower

Less than half of the people who traveled on the *Mayflower* were members of the Scrooby **congregation**. To fill up the ship, the congregation brought along people they called "strangers," who were not **Puritans**. One of the biggest challenges the **Pilgrims** faced was trying to make sure the Puritans and the strangers could get along. The Mayflower Compact was written to help unify the Puritans and the strangers.

Mayflower Passenger List

John Alden *
Isaac Allerton *
   Mary (wife) +
   Bartholomew (son)
   Remember (daughter)
   Mary (daughter)
John Allerton * +
John Billington *
   Elinor (wife)
   John (son)
   Francis (son)
William Bradford *
   Dorothy (wife) +
William Brewster *
   Mary (wife)
   Love (son)
   Wrestling (son)
Richard Britteridge * +
Peter Browne *
William Button (died during voyage)
Robert Carter +
John Carver *
   Catherine (wife)
   Dorothy (servant)
James Chilton * +
   Susanna (wife) +
   Mary (daughter)
Richard Clarke * +
Francis Cooke *
   John (son)
Humility Cooper
John Crackston * +
   John (son)
Edward Doty *

Francis Eaton *
   Sarah (wife) +
   Samuel (son)
_____ Ely
Thomas English * +
Moses Fletcher * +
Edward Fuller * +
   ___ (wife) +
   Samuel (son)
Samuel Fuller *
Richard Gardener
John Goodman * +
William Holbeck +
John Hooke +
Stephen Hopkins *
   Elizabeth (wife)
   Constance (daughter)
   Gyles (son)
   Damaris (daughter)
   Oceanus (son)
John Howland *
John Langmore +
William Latham
Edward Lester *
Edmund Margesson * +
Christopher Martin * +
   Marie (wife) +
   Solomon Prower (her son) +
Ellen Moore +
Jasper Moore +
Mary Moore +
Richard Moore
William Mullins * +
   Alice (wife) +
   Priscilla (daughter)
   Joseph (son) +

Digory Priest * +
John Rigsdale * +
   Alice (wife) +
Thomas Rogers * +
   Joseph (son)
Henry Sampson
George Soule *
Miles Standish *
   Rose (wife) +
Elias Story +
Edward Thompson +
Edward Tilley * +
   Agnes (wife) +
John Tilley * +
   Joan (wife) +
   Elizabeth (daughter)
Thomas Tinker * +
   Jane (wife) +
   ___ (son) +
William Trevore
John Turner * +
   ___ (son) +
   ___ (son) +
Richard Warren *
William White * +
   Susanna (wife)
   Resolved (son)
   Peregrine (son)
Roger Wilder +
Thomas Williams * +
Edward Winslow *
   Elizabeth (wife) +
Gilbert Winslow *

KEY:
* signed the Mayflower Compact
+ died the first winter

The Virginia Company charter

The voyage across the Atlantic Ocean was hard for the people onboard. They suffered from disease and seasickness, but only one of the 102 passengers died. When the Pilgrims sighted land at Cape Cod, Massachusetts, on November 11, 1620, they believed that the worst danger was over.

Unfortunately, the Pilgrims had landed in the wrong place. Before leaving Europe, they received a **charter** from the Virginia Company. In return for sending furs, fish, and sassafras (a kind of tree) back to Britain, the Pilgrims were given money for their trip and the rights to the land they occupied. But Massachusetts, where the *Mayflower* landed, is hundreds of miles from Virginia.

The travelers, especially the strangers, were not sure whether the rules in the Virginia Company charter still applied to them. Some of the strangers even talked about leaving the congregation to set off on their own. To prevent this, and to preserve their unity, the Pilgrims drew up the Mayflower Compact before they left the ship.

Miles Standish

Miles Standish was a soldier living in Holland when the Pilgrims left. He was not a member of the Scrooby congregation, but was taken on as the community's military leader. He was the most powerful of the "strangers." His willingness to cooperate with the Puritan leaders helped hold the **colony** together. It was Miles Standish who discovered a large stockpile of corn that helped the Pilgrims survive the first winter. He also played a large role in keeping relations peaceful between the Pilgrims, the Wampanoags, and other Native Americans living in the area.

The long journey across the Atlantic Ocean was just the beginning of the Pilgrims' hardships.

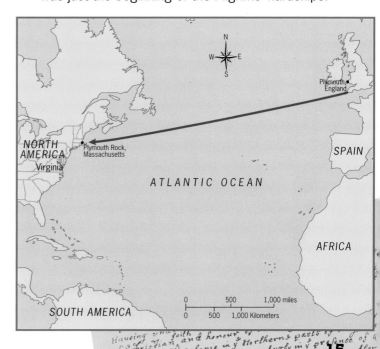

William Brewster

One of the leaders of the Scrooby **congregation** and authors of the Mayflower Compact was a man named William Brewster. Brewster's home in Scrooby was the group's original meeting place. Although he was not their religious leader, he always played an important role in the group. He also became a kind of second father to William Bradford, the future leader of Plymouth **Colony.**

In Leiden, Holland, Brewster was the church's **deacon** and **elder.** He was the only church official to make the first trip to the New World. Once there, he led religious services until 1629. Brewster probably played a large part in writing the Mayflower Compact, since he had a lot of experience with these kinds of documents.

William Brewster was a strong and influential force in Plymouth Colony.

Know It

The average age of the *Mayflower* passengers was around 34.

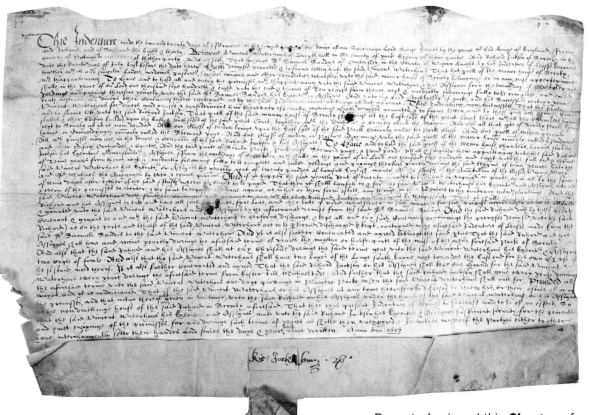

Brewster's signed this **Charter** of Massachusetts Bay from 1629. Even at that time, he was still active in the colony's future.

Separatist churches often drew up **covenants** to declare their unity and independence. No one knows who actually chose the words in the Mayflower Compact and wrote them down, but Brewster would have been a natural choice to do much of the work. After the **colonists** settled in America, Brewster became Governor Bradford's main advisor, although he never held a political office.

John Carver

John Carver was a wealthy **merchant** from Doncaster, England, which is ten miles (sixteen kilometers) north of Scrooby. He had invested most of his fortune in the *Mayflower* journey—more than anyone else. Because of his wealth and seniority, he was chosen as the first governor of the new colony shortly after the colonists signed the Mayflower Compact. He helped convince the strangers to stay with the colony after he became governor. Carver was not governor for very long. He died in April 1621.

The Mayflower Compact

THE FIRST DECLARATION OF THE PRINCIPLES OF AMERICAN FREEDOM

17

William Bradford

Another important figure in the writing of the Mayflower Compact was William Bradford. His parents were farmers in northern England. Bradford joined the Scrooby **congregation** and moved with them to Leiden, Holland, in 1609. He became a weaver in Leiden and raised a family. After arriving in the New World, he was elected governor after John Carver died. Over the next 45 years, Bradford was chosen as governor almost every single year. The **colony** elected someone else only five times!

Bradford was a strong and successful leader of Plymouth Colony.

John Winthrop

John Winthrop was the first governor and **historian** of the Massachusetts Bay Colony. It was located to the north of Plymouth Colony, near what is now Boston. He came from a wealthy family in Suffolk, England, and was a **devout Puritan.** He came to the New World in 1629, after losing a lot of money in an **economic depression.** He served as governor of Massachusetts Bay Colony twelve times between 1629 and 1649 and was known as a strict, but mostly fair ruler. His written history of New England was not published until the nineteenth century.

Bradford's optimism and encouragement helped the **colonists** survive the first winter, when half of the **Pilgrims** died. He helped promote peace with the neighboring Native Americans. He also demanded that the Colony stay united, rather than break into smaller groups. After the Massachusetts Bay Colony was **founded** in 1630 by John Winthrop and another group of Puritans, Bradford struggled to keep Plymouth Colony separate and independent from its larger neighbor.

Samoset and Squanto

Samoset and Squanto were members of the Wampanoags, the Native American group living closest to Plymouth Colony. They had each encountered earlier English explorers in the area. Squanto even lived in London for several years. Because they knew English, they acted as messengers between their chief, Massasoit, and the colonists. Samoset and Squanto also taught the newcomers farming and fishing secrets that helped them survive in the New World. For 40 years, the Native Americans and the Puritans lived together rather peacefully. Samoset and Squanto helped make this time of peace possible.

The Historian of Plymouth

No one knows where the original copy of the Mayflower Compact is located. It was possibly stolen from the Old South Church in Boston during the **Revolutionary War.** However it is more likely that the original document has simply not survived. That means the first known handwritten copy of the Mayflower Compact is actually in a book written by William Bradford.

The first historian

William Bradford was not just a political leader—he was also the New World's first **historian.** His book, *Of Plymouth Plantation,* is the source of most of what we know about the early **Pilgrims.** His book tells the entire story of the Pilgrims' life in Holland, their decision to travel to the New World, and their arrival off Cape Cod, Massachusetts, in November, 1620. Bradford described their living arrangements and some of the problems they faced.

Part of the book is a diary where Bradford recorded his feelings year after year. Toward the end of his life, Bradford grew somewhat unhappy

This is a **replica** of the first page from Governor Bradford's book, *Of Plymouth Plantation.* He tried to include as many details about the Pilgrims' experience as possible.

Bradford diary entry

In his book, Bradford described the mood of the people as they approached land:

> After many difficulties in boisterous [powerful] storms, at length by God's providence . . . we espied [spotted] land, which we deemed to be Cape Cod . . . and upon the 21 of November we came to anchor in the bay [Provincetown Harbor]. . . .
>
> Occasioned partly by the discontented [unhappy] and mutinous [rebellious] speeches that some of the strangers amongst them had let fall from them [spoken] in the ship; that when they came ashore they would use their own liberty, for none had power to command them, the **patent** they had being for Virginia and not for New England, which belonged to another government, with which the Virginia Company had nothing to do . . .

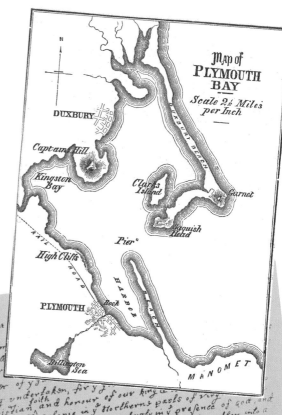

This is an early map of Plymouth Colony. Plymouth Rock is also highlighted.

because he felt the old traditions of Plymouth **Colony** were disappearing. He feared that eventually the Colony would be absorbed by the Massachusetts Bay Colony. This in fact happened in 1692.

Not only does Bradford's book contain the first written copy of the Mayflower Compact, but it also contains a description of why it was written. He explains that the strangers claimed that onshore they "would use their own liberty; for none had power to command them." In other words, they would not follow the rules set by the **Puritans,** since the Virginia Company **charter** was not valid in Massachusetts. The Mayflower Compact was written to make sure everyone cooperated and followed certain rules.

Laws and Covenants

The Mayflower Compact was primarily a legal document. Today, laws are written down in books and are enforced by police and courts. But in the seventeenth century, things were more complicated. The rules were not the same everywhere. For example, onboard a ship the master or captain was in charge. Whatever he believed was best for the ship was the law. That is why it was important for the **Pilgrims** to sign the Mayflower Compact before leaving the ship. Onboard the *Mayflower*, the master, Christopher Jones, was responsible for making and enforcing the law, but once on land the Pilgrims had nothing to guide them.

The Mayflower covenant

The idea of a **covenant** was important to groups like the Scrooby **congregation** and they had some experience writing their own laws. Because they wanted to live a strict and religiously pure life, they had rules that were different from those of the people around them. For instance,

Pilgrims attend a service at the first church in New England.

many **Puritan** groups did not allow dancing, and punished any member of the community who danced. These rules were part of the covenants such religious groups often wrote, and William Brewster and many of the other members were very familiar with them. Covenants helped small religious groups stay independent from the people living around them.

Text of the Mayflower Compact

The text of the Mayflower Compact can be difficult for many to read. That is because the spelling and the language itself has changed since the Compact was written. However, one can still follow the ideas of the Compact:

These are the signatures of some of the men who signed the Mayflower Compact.

In ye name of God, Amen., We whose names are underwritten, the loyall subjects of our dread soveraigne Lord, King James, by the grace of God, of Great Britaine, Franc, and Ireland king, defender of the faith, etc.

Haveing undertaken, for ye glorie of God, and advancemente of ye Christain faith, and honour of our king & countrie, a voyage to plant ye first colonie in ye Northerne parts of Virginia, doe by these presents solemnly & mutualy in ye presence of God, and one of another, covenant & combine our selves togeather into a civill body politik, for our better ordering & preservation & furtherance of ye ends aforesaid; and by vertue hearof to enacte lawes, ordinances, acts constitutions, & offices, from time to time, as shall be thought most meet & convenient for ye generall good of ye Colonie, unto which we promise all due submission and obedience. In witnes wherof we have hereunder subscribed our names at Cap-Codd ye 11th. of November, in ye year of ye raigne of our soveraigne lord, King James, of England, France, & Ireland ye eighteenth, and of Scotland, ye fiftie fourth. Ano: Dom. 1620.

Mourt's Relation

After arriving in the New World, the **Pilgrims** encountered tremendous difficulties. They landed just as winter was about to begin, and they had to work quickly to find food and shelter in order to survive. Miles Standish found a large amount of corn that had been abandoned by Native Americans, but the **colonists** were still struck hard by disease. Only 4 of the 102 travelers avoided falling ill, and almost half of the Pilgrims died during that first winter.

From letters and diaries to book

William Bradford and one of his close friends, Edward Winslow, kept a record of those early years to send back to England. They wanted to let people know about their experiences, and reassure their loved ones that they were still alive and safe. In 1622, a book was published in London made up of their letters and diary entries. The book was called *Mourt's Relation,* and most of it was written by Winslow. It is an important document because it contains a version of the Mayflower Compact.

Edward Winslow

Edward Winslow joined John Robinson's **congregation** in 1617 in Leiden, Holland, where he worked with William Brewster as a printer. After coming to America, he was an important messenger between the new **colony** and England. He frequently traveled back and forth, helping to convince more members to join the colony. He also helped settle the financial and legal problems of Plymouth Colony. In 1651, Winslow's portrait was drawn by an English painter, probably Robert Walker. He is the only Pilgrim to be painted or drawn during his lifetime. For the others, we have to guess what they looked like.

In fact, this is the oldest version of the Compact, since Bradford's handwritten copy was actually written later. Usually, the earliest known handwritten version of a document is older than the first printed edition, but in the case of the Mayflower Compact the reverse is true.

Compact wording

The wording of the Compact is the same in *Mourt's Relation* and in William Bradford's book, *Of Plymouth Plantation*. A third version of the Compact appears in a book written by Bradford's nephew, Nathaniel Morton, called *New England's Memorial*. The words in this text are also the same, but what is different is the number of people who signed the document. In Bradford and Winslow's versions around 65 people signed, while Morton lists only 41. Morton is probably right. Bradford and Winslow listed all of the men on board the ship, but they did not all sign the Compact. Some of the men were servants or *Mayflower* sailors, and their votes did not count. Bradford and Winslow wrote down their names because they wanted to have a record of all the men who sailed and were part of the colony. Women and children were not allowed to sign the Compact.

Bradford wrote out the Mayflower Compact in his book.

Bradford's Copy of the Mayflower Compact

This painting shows the signing of the Mayflower Compact aboard the ship. No one left the ship until after the Compact was signed.

Bradford copied down the Mayflower Compact in such a way that it would last a very long time. Even though it was lost for many years, and moved back and forth between the United States and England, the book is still in extremely good condition. Bradford used paper made of rags rather than wood pulp, which is what paper is made of now. The rags are very sturdy, and only some pages have small rips or tears in them. The book was beautifully bound in vellum, or calf-skin leather. It is light brown in color and has **warped** a little over the years.

Spelling

Something that one notices right away if one reads the original copy of the Mayflower Compact is that it is hard to understand. That is because words were spelled differently in the seventeenth century than they are today. For example, the authors of the Compact agreed "by vertue hearof to enacte lawes, ordinances, act constitutions, & offices . . ." The word "vertue" is now spelled "virtue"; "enacte" is now "enact" and "lawes" is now "laws." The Compact also spells "having" as "haveing" and "the" as "ye." Eventually, words took the form by which we spell them today. But even then, some **primary source** documents were still spelled in unusual ways.

Standardized spelling did not come into wide use until the first dictionaries were published. In the United States, this happened in the nineteenth century, when Noah Webster's dictionary became popular and cheap enough that people could buy one for their homes.

In ye name of God, Amen., We whose names are underwritten, the loyall subjects of our dread soveraigne Lord, King James, by the grace of God, of Great Britaine, Franc, and Ireland king, defender of the faith, etc. Haveing undertaken, for ye glorie of God, and advancemente of ye Christain faith, and honour of our king & countrie, a voyage to plant ye first colonie in ye Northerne parts of Virginia, doe by these presents solemnly & mutualy in ye presence of God, and one of . . .

In this small passage from the Mayflower Compact, almost half of the words are spelled differently than they are today. This difference can make reading the document difficult.

Plymouth or Plimouth?

The spelling for Plymouth **Colony** varied depending on who was doing the writing. In various documents from the time period, Plymouth has been spelled "Plimouth," "Plymoth," "Plimoth," or just "Plim."

Loyal to the King

The Mayflower Compact was both a religious and a political document. It begins with a standard opening in seventeenth-century **proclamations**, "In the name of God, Amen." The Compact goes on to state that the signers of the document consider themselves "loyall subjects of our dread [fearful] soveraigne Lord King James, by the grace of God, of Great Britaine, Franc, and Ireland king." James was King of England—or Great Britain—in 1620. It is strange that the **Pilgrims** claimed

This painting depicts the Pilgrim families gathered around their pastor, John Robinson, for a farewell service on the deck of the *Speedwell* before its departure from Holland.

James I

James I was king of Great Britain from 1603 to 1625. He was not a well-loved king, but his reign is known for some of its great literary achievements. For instance, King James collected some of the best writers in the country to produce a new translation of the Bible. This is still known today as the *King James Bible*. He also supported the playwright William Shakespeare and invited him to write and perform new works for his court.

to be loyal subjects of the king. After all, they had fled the country back in 1609 to avoid persecution by the government. But the Pilgrims had received money and support from the British government, and so they felt they had to proclaim their **loyalty** to the king.

King of France?

It might also seem unusual that the Pilgrims called James king not only of Great Britain and Ireland, but also of France. During the **Middle Ages,** the English kings had owned large pieces of land in France. They only lost the land after a bloody series of battles known as the Hundred Years' War. Even though the British had lost their lands in France, they still believed they had a right to them. That is why James was addressed as king of France.

The Hundred Years' War

The Hundred Years' War lasted from 1337 to 1453. It covered the reigns of five British and five French kings. In the fighting, the British won most of the battles, however the French won the war. Joan of Arc played a major role in helping the French win. She led a French army to end a siege of Orléans in 1429. She became a prisoner of the British, who later burned her to death.

A "Civil Body Politic"

The Mayflower Compact goes on to declare that the signers "**covenant** & combine our selves togeather into a civill body politik." The **Pilgrims** thought of themselves as a religious group, but also thought of their group as a political body, or a "civil body politic." This means that they would form their own government and their own laws. Thus no one person would tell the others what to do. They would make decisions together. All members of the **colony** would be expected to obey these laws and participate in governing the land they occupied. The Compact grants the **colonists** the right to create "lawes, ordinances [armies], acts constitutions, & offices" which will be most "convenient for ye generall good of ye colonie." The Pilgrims knew that they would survive and preserve their colony only if they cooperated with each other.

Stay united

The Pilgrims wanted to be sure that no member of the group believed he could do whatever he wanted. Some of the strangers had earlier expressed an interest in living on their own, and the other colonists insisted that the group remain united. Therefore, any law agreed to by the colonial government would have to be followed by everyone. This was the most important achievement of the Mayflower Compact. It made sure that the rule of law would triumph in the New World, rather than chaos and disorder.

A Native American watches as the *Mayflower* reaches shore at Cape Cod, Massachusetts.

Supposedly, Mary Chilton was the first person to set foot on Plymouth Rock. However, there is no historical fact that supports this claim.

It has sometimes been claimed that the Compact was more than this. In the nineteenth century it was especially believed that the Compact was a radically new invention that paved the way for the United States **Constitution** 150 years later. But this is not really true. John Robinson, the pastor of the Scrooby **congregation**, wrote a letter to the Pilgrims before they left Plymouth and urged them to adopt a covenant once they reached the New World. He wanted to be sure that they made decisions as a group. These kinds of agreements, therefore, were already well-known in the seventeenth century.

Importance of a covenant

The Mayflower Compact was extremely important—the passengers of the *Mayflower* needed to stay together in a "civil body politic." The Mayflower Compact is what allowed them to do this. The Compact was signed aboard the *Mayflower* on November 22, 1620, by 41 men. At the time, Governor William Bradford stated:

This day, before we came to harbour, observing some not well affected to unity and concord [harmony], but gave some appearance of faction [a group], it was thought good there should be an association and agreement, that we should combine together in one body, and to submit to such government and governors as we should by common consent agree to make and choose, and set our hands to this that follows, word for word . . .

The Mayflower
THE FIRST DECLARATION OF THE PRINCIPLES OF AMERICA

Preserving Unity

▲ Religion was a large part of the **Pilgrims'** lives. As shown in this painting, the Pilgrims did not need a church in order to hold worship.

The Mayflower Compact and the ideas it stood for were tested greatly during the early years of Plymouth **Colony.** Miles Standish helped make sure that the colony stayed unified. In 1623, he rescued a group of settlers near starvation who were employees of a man named Thomas Weston. In 1624, he settled a dispute with another **"particular"** named John Oldham. Finally, in 1628, he closed down Thomas Morton's trading post at Merry Mount, where some **colonists** were violating the **moral** rules of the Colony. Standish's military abilities were very important in making sure that everyone followed the Mayflower Compact and other laws and agreements like it.

Mayflower Compact short-lived

As important as it was in keeping the early colonists united, the Mayflower Compact was only used for about six months. After the Pilgrims' first winter was over, the *Mayflower* and its crew returned to Great Britain. There they explained to the government that the ship had sailed off course and landed in Massachusetts instead of Virginia. Since its Virginia Company **charter** was no longer valid, the King issued something called the Peirce **Patent** in the summer of 1621. It became the new legal documents for Plymouth Colony.

It gave the colonists a right to the land they occupied and set rules which they had to follow. Every year they elected a governor, but the whole community had a say in the decisions that were made.

The Peirce Patent

John Peirce led a group of Plymouth **merchants** to the Council for New England in London. His goal was to obtain permission for the colonists to settle in New England. In 1621, the Peirce Patent replaced the Mayflower Compact, and gave the Pilgrims the right to settle in Plymouth.

The Loss of Bradford's Book

Boston's Old South Church is shown in this photograph from 1900.

As the American **colonies** developed, people did not pay much attention to the Mayflower Compact. Bradford's *Of Plymouth Plantation* was not published for many years, and only a few **historians** were able to read his manuscript. The book was stored in the Old South Church in Boston, Massachusetts. Early American historians consulted it to learn about the first years of Plymouth Colony. Sometimes these historians would reprint the Compact as an **appendix** to their books, but many people had simply forgotten it.

Then, during the **Revolutionary War,** the British army invaded Boston and several items were stolen from the Old South Church. One of the items may have been the original copy of the Mayflower Compact. It has never been found. Bradford's book was also stolen and for many years it was believed to have been lost too. In 1855, the book was discovered in London in a bishop's library. After many years, it was returned to the governor of Massachusetts, and that is why it is stored in the Massachusetts State House today.

Increased interest in the Compact

Even before Bradford's book was located, people in the nineteenth century were paying a lot more attention to the **Pilgrims** of Plymouth. After the United States **Constitution** was adopted in 1789, the early **colonists** no longer seemed like British **subjects** seeking to live in the New World, but future Americans struggling for independence.

Two important figures who described the Mayflower Compact as a **foreshadowing** of the U.S. Constitution and the **Declaration of Independence** were James Wilson and John Quincy Adams. Today, historians believe that Wilson and Adams exaggerated the importance of the Compact. But Wilson and Adams performed a valuable service in reminding people of this interesting part of American history.

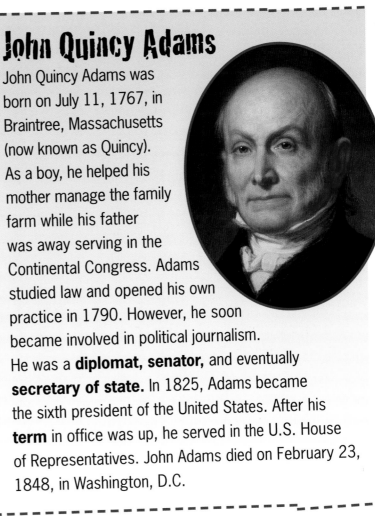

James Wilson

James Wilson was born in Scotland in 1742. He moved to America in 1765 and became a successful lawyer in Carlisle, Pennsylvania. Wilson was only one of six people to sign both the Declaration of Independence and the U.S. Constitution. In 1789, he was appointed to the U.S. **Supreme Court.** Wilson died in 1798.

John Quincy Adams

John Quincy Adams was born on July 11, 1767, in Braintree, Massachusetts (now known as Quincy). As a boy, he helped his mother manage the family farm while his father was away serving in the Continental Congress. Adams studied law and opened his own practice in 1790. However, he soon became involved in political journalism. He was a **diplomat, senator,** and eventually **secretary of state.** In 1825, Adams became the sixth president of the United States. After his **term** in office was up, he served in the U.S. House of Representatives. John Adams died on February 23, 1848, in Washington, D.C.

John and Priscilla Alden

A poet named Henry Wadsworth Longfellow played an especially big role in drawing attention to the history of the **Pilgrims.** In 1842 he published a long poem, *The Courtship of Miles Standish,* which did more to revive excitement about the Pilgrims and the Mayflower Compact than anything else.

Henry Wadsworth Longfellow

The poem is about two friends, Miles Standish and John Alden. Standish is described as an older man whose entire life has been devoted to war. Alden, meanwhile, is portrayed as a young and very handsome man, who is well-educated. Alden is secretly in love with Priscilla, a young woman living in Plymouth **Colony** whose relatives all died in the winter of 1621. One day, Standish tells Alden that he would like to marry Priscilla, and asks Alden to ask her on his behalf. Alden feels he must do as his friend requests, despite his own feelings for Priscilla. But when he urges her to marry Miles Standish, she responds, "Why don't you speak for yourself, John?" Basically, she asks why John does not propose to her.

When Alden tells Standish what happened he is furious, and accuses his friend of betraying him. For many months they do not speak. Suddenly, one day news arrives that Standish has been killed in battle. Alden and Priscilla now feel free to marry each other. At the wedding Standish appears, alive and well, and apologizes for his anger and stubbornness.

Longfellow's poem has no basis in fact, but it was so popular that it sparked new interest in Plymouth Colony. This helped make more people aware of the status of the Mayflower Compact in our early history.

John and Priscilla Alden watch the *Mayflower* disappear into the distance on its journey back to England.

The "real" John Alden

The real John Alden was very different from the character in Longfellow's poem. Alden lived in Southhampton, England, where the *Mayflower* stopped in 1620 for supplies. He was hired as the ship's **cooper.** Alden was responsible for the ship's beer and drinking water. Once they arrived in the New World, Alden became an important member of the colony. One reason he has become famous is that many of his descendants were also well-known people. John Adams, the second president of the United States, was related to Alden, and so was Henry Wadsworth Longfellow himself!

How Thanksgiving Became a Holiday

We celebrate Thanksgiving every November to remember the **Pilgrims,** who after surviving their first year in the New World, threw a great feast. Following the advice of Squanto, the **colonists** placed a fish next to each kernel of corn they planted. The result was a huge crop that would help them survive in Plymouth permanently. To thank the Wampanoags for their help, the Pilgrims invited them to a dinner that lasted for several days. But they did not eat turkey, cranberries, or pumpkin pie. They probably ate ducks, geese, venison, oysters, and lobster.

One-time Thanksgiving

Many people assume that this made Thanksgiving a holiday, but in fact the feast was not repeated in the following years. As the American **colonies** grew, and especially after the **Revolutionary War,** many New

Who attended the first Thanksgiving?

Around 52 colonists attended the first Thanksgiving. Among the colonists were Miles Standish, William Bradford, Isaac Allerton, and John Alden. The only Native American that we know for certain attended the first

Thanksgiving in 1621 was Massasoit. However, it is likely that Squanto was there. Three other Native Americans also may have been present: Hobbamock, Quadequina (Massasoit's brother), and Tokamahamon. Samoset was probably not in the area at this time.

Englanders began celebrating "Forefathers' Day" in December. Forefathers' Day honored all the early settlers in America. Some presidents, including George Washington, created one-time Thanksgiving holidays to remember the Pilgrims' first feast. But it was not until 1865 that Abraham Lincoln made it a permanent holiday. Even then, it was celebrated mostly by people living in the northeastern United States, or New England.

Abraham Lincoln

Thanksgiving is official

Thanksgiving came to be celebrated in its present form by most Americans in about 1900. Thanksgiving probably would not be a major holiday at all if people during the nineteenth century had not started paying more attention to the Mayflower Compact and the people who wrote it.

Plymouth Rock

Another part of the Pilgrims' story that was "rediscovered" after being forgotten for many years is the legend of Plymouth Rock. The colonists probably did not pay much attention to Plymouth Rock when they first landed. Later generations, however, claimed it was the spot where the Pilgrims first landed and turned it into a tourist attraction. During the Revolutionary War, a group of people celebrating the anniversary of the *Mayflower* voyage tried to move the rock. It broke in half and stayed that way for more than 100 years.

Interview with an Archivist

Betsy Lowenstein is an **archivist** in the Special Collections department at the Massachusetts State House Library, where the first copy of the Mayflower Compact is stored.

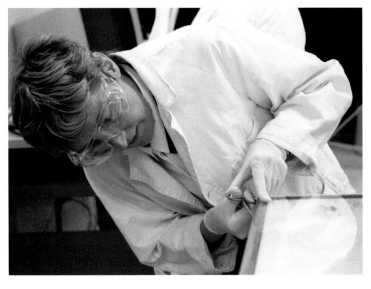

Archivists must be very careful when working with **primary source** materials.

How did you decide to become an archivist?

I've always been interested in history and in fact began work toward a Master's degree in History before deciding that the degree would be too limiting. **Archival** work provided a bit more flexibility. In working with historical records, I would be able to satisfy my interest in history and research, but there would be greater career options for me; I would be more "employable" (or so I hoped).

What is a typical day like in your office?

As a department head, I run the Special Collections department at the State Library. Every day I work a two-hour shift at the reference desk, answering questions and pulling materials for researchers. There are always large ongoing projects such as creating the library's first preservation plan, updating an obsolete [out of date] disaster plan, cataloging uncataloged manuscripts, or writing a grant for the digitization [transferring documents to computer] of a significant manuscript collection (I'm involved in the last now). On a smaller level, I respond to correspondence; arrange for the photo-reproduction of a photograph or map, whatever item a patron

The Massachusetts State House Library stores the Mayflower Compact as well as other important historical documents.

may request; or give tours to the staff of a **legislator** or, in the summer, legislative **interns.** In the fall and spring, I supervise interns from a local archives program in the processing of archival collections.

What is your most memorable accomplishment?

In my previous job, I oversaw the design, construction, and furnishing of a state-of-the-art research library. I am most proud of this achievement as I had never been involved before in a building project—there was a tremendous learning curve—and work occurred while I was managing an existing library. If the digitization project I mentioned above is completed successfully, this will be another memorable accomplishment.

Become an archivist

Interested in history and science? Consider becoming an archivist or document **conservator.** Archivists and document conservators have to be good at working with their hands, because they do detailed work on old documents that must be carefully handled. Some knowledge of science is important, too. Those who do this work must be aware of how different chemicals interact in various environments. Besides working with papers and books, archivists could work with photographs, **textiles,** furniture, and other items.

The Mayflower Compact Today

Bradford's manuscript is only handled once or twice a year. Sometimes **scholars** are allowed to see the original manuscript for their research. Often, they are looking for things that cannot be seen in a printed copy or photocopy. Sometimes they simply want to get a sense of the look and feel of the original document. Massachusetts state **senators** and representatives also have the right to view the document if they wish.

Protecting the Compact

When not being handled, Bradford's book is stored in a highly secure and climate-controlled area. The temperature is constantly kept at 65°F (18°C) and 42% **humidity.** The book is wrapped in acid-tissue and placed in a clamshell box to protect it from light. Until 1984, *Of Plymouth Plantation* was displayed in a glass case in the Massachusetts

The Massachusetts State Archives is located in Boston.

State **Archives.** To protect the paper and ink from the effects of light, the **archivists** moved it into safe storage. Occasionally the manuscript has been loaned to museums for temporary display.

Bradford's book is in extremely good condition. Since the paper is made from rags, it has survived its many travels with little damage. The paper is stained and dirty in some places, but still easy to read. The page containing the Mayflower Compact is darker than the other pages because it was on display for several years and collected extra dirt and dust during that period. The ink has hardly faded at all, although in some places it has bled through the page. Given the careful way it is handled, the oldest version of the Mayflower Compact should be with us for many more generations.

Read the Mayflower Compact

The text of the Mayflower Compact is reproduced on several websites on the Internet. Some websites provide background information or explain what the Compact means. Read the Mayflower Compact and see who signed it at www.plimoth.org/Library/compact.htm.

A Model of Plymouth Colony

Plymouth **Colony** disappeared a long time ago. Today, the city of Plymouth stands in the area where the **Pilgrims** first settled. For the most part it is like any other town. One organization, however, has tried to keep the memory of the Pilgrims alive. The Plimoth Society—*Plimoth* is the original spelling of Plymouth—has even built a reproduction of what the village looked like in the days of William Bradford and Miles Standish. Houses, streets, crops, and tools have been reproduced as they were in 1627.

Plimoth Plantation is a **replica** of the original Plymouth settlement.

Know It

Visit Plymouth on the Internet at www.plimoth.org. This website features a virtual tour of Plymouth Colony, along with facts about life during that time.

The *Mayflower II* is a replica of the ship that brought the Pilgrims to the New World. It can be found in Plymouth Harbor, Massachusetts.

Visitors to the Plimoth Society can eat the same foods the Pilgrims did and see crafts produced just as they were in the 1620s. One exhibit shows how a Wampanoag counselor and warrior named Hobbamock lived. The Plimoth Society also holds festivals and other events to honor and remember the Pilgrims. An exact copy of the *Mayflower* was built in 1957 and stands in Plymouth Harbor.

We owe many important things in our culture to the Pilgrims: the Thanksgiving holiday, Plymouth Rock, and Henry Wadsworth Longfellow's *The Courtship of Miles Standish* are some of the most memorable. But we should remember that the greatest achievement of the **colonists** was to insist that in their society, decisions be made in common. No one was above the law, and no one could govern the people without their consent. This is the lasting message of the Mayflower Compact.

Glossary

appendix part of a book giving added and helpful information

archive place in which public records or historical papers are stored

archivist person who works to restore and preserve public records and historical papers

broadside large sheet of paper printed on one side

charter official document granting, guaranteeing, or showing the limits of the rights and duties of the group to which it is given

clergy group of religious officials (such as priests, ministers, or rabbis) specially prepared and authorized to lead religious services

colonist person who lives in a colony

colony settlement in a new territory that is tied to an established nation

congregation assembly of persons gathered especially for religious worship; membership of a church or synagogue

conservator person who is responsible for the care, restoration, and repair of documents and other historical artifacts

constitution document that outlines the basic principles of a government

convert change from one belief, religion, view, or party to another. A person who has been converted is a *convert*.

cooper worker who makes or repairs wooden casks, tubs, or barrels

covenant agreement in which a religious community binds itself together

debate argument that follows certain rules

Declaration of Independence document in which the American colonies formally declared independence from Great Britain in 1776

deacon church member who has special duties, such as helping a priest or minister

devout devoted to religion

diplomat person sent by one government to negotiate with another

economic depression period of low general economic activity, especially marked by rising levels of unemployment

elder person who has authority because of age and experience; official in some churches

estate fine country house on a large piece of land

foreshadow indicate beforehand

found start something, like a school

historian person who studies or writes about history

humidity amount of moisture, or water, in the air

intern student in a professional field that gains experience outside the classroom, such as in a hospital or museum

journal written record of daily events

legislator person who makes laws

legislature group of elected individuals who make laws for those who elect them

loyalty being faithful to one's country or personal beliefs

merchant store owner or trader

Middle Ages period of European history from about 500 C.E. to about 1500

monk member of a religious group of men who form a community and promise to stay poor, obey all the laws of their community, and not get married

moral concerned with or relating to what is right and wrong in human behavior; good or virtuous

pamphlet booklet with no cover, usually made of paper folded into smaller parts

particular someone who had the right to live outside Plymouth Colony and did not have to follow its laws

patent document that gives a person or group of people permission to do something

Pilgrim one of the British colonists who founded the first permanent settlement in New England at Plymouth in 1620

pope head of the Roman Catholic Church

primary source original copy of a journal, letter, newspaper, document, or image

proclamation act of announcing publicly

Protestant Reformation time in Europe during the 1500s when groups began to spilt from the Catholic Church and form new religions

Puritan member of a religious group that settled in New England in the sixteenth and seventeenth centuries; Puritans rejected the services of the Church of England

radical departing sharply from the usual or ordinary; extreme

replica exact copy

Revolutionary War American fight for independence from British rule between 1775 and 1783

scholar student; person who knows a great deal about one or more subjects

secondary source written account of an event by someone who studied a primary source or sources

secretary of state person in the U.S. government who is responsible for foreign affairs

senator member of a legislative branch in a government

Separatist strict religious group that wanted to live entirely on their own, with their own church, schools, and government

sin action that breaks a religious law

standardize set up as a rule or as a model; regularly and widely used

subject person under the authority or control of another

Supreme Court highest court of the U.S. consisting of a chief justice and eight associate justices

term period of time fixed by law

textile item made from woven cloth

warp curve or twist out of shape

More Books to Read

Apel, Melanie Ann. *The Pilgrims.* Farmington Hills, Mich.: Gale Group, 2003.

Arenstam, Peter, John Kemp, and Catherine ONeill Grace. *Mayflower 1620: A New Look at an Early Colonial Voyage.* Washington, D.C.: National Geographic Society, 2003.

Whitcraft, Melissa. *The Mayflower Compact.* Danbury, Conn.: Children's Press, 2003.

Index